GALAXY OF SUPERSTARS

Ben Affleck
Backstreet Boys
Brandy
Garth Brooks
Mariah Carey
Matt Damon
Cameron Diaz
Leonardo DiCaprio
Céline Dion
Tom Hanks
Hanson
Jennifer Love Hewitt
Lauryn Hill
Jennifer Lopez
Ricky Martin
Ewan McGregor
Mike Myers
'N Sync
LeAnn Rimes
Adam Sandler
Britney Spears
Spice Girls
Jonathan Taylor Thomas
Venus Williams

CHELSEA HOUSE PUBLISHERS

THE AMERICAN MUSIC AWARDS
AMA
THE AMERICAN MUSIC AWARDS
AMERICAN MUSIC AWARD

GALAXY OF SUPERSTARS

Céline Dion

Norma Jean Lutz

CHELSEA HOUSE PUBLISHERS
Philadelphia

Frontis: *Céline Dion's charismatic stage presence and powerful voice catapulted her to the top of the music industry, winning her almost every major music award.*

Produced by
21st Century Publishing and Communications, Inc.
New York, New York
http://www.21cpc.com

CHELSEA HOUSE PUBLISHERS

Editor in Chief: Stephen Reginald
Managing Editor: James D. Gallagher
Production Manager: Pamela Loos
Art Director: Sara Davis
Director of Photography: Judy L. Hasday
Senior Production Editor: J. Christopher Higgins
Publishing Coordinator/Project Editor: James McAvoy

The Chelsea House World Wide Web address is
http://www.chelseahouse.com

First Printing

1 3 5 7 9 8 6 4 2

Library of Congress Cataloging-in-Publication Data

Lutz, Norma Jean.
    Céline Dion / by Norma Jean Lutz.
        p. cm. — (Galaxy of superstars)
    Includes bibliographical references (p. 63) and index.
    Summary: A biography of the French Canadian pop singer known for her
hit single "My Heart Will Go On," the theme song from the movie "Titanic."
    ISBN 0-7910-5777-1 — ISBN 0-7910-5778-X (pbk.)
    1. Dion, Céline—Juvenile literature. 2. Singers—Canada—Biography—
Juvenile literature. [1. Dion, Céline. 2. Singers. 3. Women—Biography.]
I. Title. II. Series.

ML3930.D47 L88 2000
782.42164'092—dc21
[B]   99-462034
                                                                                  CIP
                                                                                  AC

CONTENTS

SETTING PRECEDENTS
AT THE ACADEMY AWARDS

The very first Academy Awards were presented to deserving entertainers on May 16, 1929. It was the year after talking pictures arrived on the scene. From its small beginning—250 in attendance—to the present, the event excites moviegoers with high levels of anticipation.

For years, awards night dazzled spectators who crowded about to catch a glimpse of glamorous stars and starlets arriving in shiny limousines, decked out in furs and diamonds. It's the night to "see and be seen."

Just such a spectacle took place in front of the castle-like Shrine Auditorium in Los Angeles, California, on awards night, March 24, 1997. From one limousine emerged a 28-year-old Canadian singer by the name of Céline Dion. Her silvery sequined designer dress was accented with a unique comet-shaped neckpiece set with more than 600 diamonds. The sight of the slender beauty turned many heads as she and her husband and manager, René Angélil, walked hand-in-hand up the red carpet and into the auditorium.

Céline, a small-town girl from Canada, had from early childhood dreamed of becoming a famous singer. Her life

Céline Dion wowed an estimated one billion TV viewers with her inspired, history-making performances of two songs nominated for Best Original Song at the 1997 Academy Awards ceremony.

to this point had convinced her that dreams can come true. And on this night, not only was she mingling with some of the most famous stars in the world, but she would also make Academy Awards history.

For years, Céline had remained a household name in her home province of Quebec. However, breaking in as a headliner in the United States had proven more difficult. But after years of hard work, Céline had succeeded, and in 1997, she was one of the most popular performers in North America.

Her recording of "Because You Loved Me," the love theme from the movie *Up Close and Personal*, had been featured in nearly every TV ad for the movie. Extensive advertising credits pushed the song into the number one spot. Because it was nominated for an Oscar for Best Original Song (a songwriter's award), Céline received an invitation to perform the number live at the awards ceremony, which she happily accepted.

Also up for an award was the song "I Finally Found Someone" from the Barbra Streisand film *The Mirror Has Two Faces*. Streisand, Céline's idol for many years, worked on the song as a cowriter. Streisand's song was to be performed by Natalie Cole. Unfortunately, the day before the awards ceremony, Natalie Cole came down with the flu and called to say she could not appear.

Show producers, who were pressed into immediate action, turned to Céline, asking if she might sing the number in Natalie's place. Never in the history of the Academy Awards had any entertainer performed two numbers at the ceremony. Because of Céline's intense admiration of Barbra Streisand, and because she was excited to make academy history, she quickly agreed.

Since there was no time to rehearse the number, Céline had but one request. She asked that the words to the song be placed on a music stand near her, in addition to being displayed on the large TelePrompTer. This would ease her nerves as she sang the unfamiliar lyrics before an estimated one billion TV viewers.

Céline did not know that Barbra Streisand herself sat in the audience that evening. She'd thought since Streisand was not singing her own song, she must not be in attendance.

When host Billy Crystal introduced Céline, the audience of more than 6,000 received her warmly. Both numbers were performed with Céline's usual power-packed emotion. Both came off without a hitch.

Hollywood has long been famous for rumors that fly about at the speed of light. When Céline sang the first few notes of Barbra Streisand's song, the famous singer got up and walked out of the auditorium. Some said she simply made a trip to the ladies' room. The gossipy tabloids, however, accused Streisand of being upset at her song being performed by a younger singer. And a Canadian at that.

Which story is true, perhaps only Streisand knows. The fact is that Streisand later sent a bouquet of flowers and a kind note to Céline. The note commended Céline's performance and added, "Next time, let's do one together."

While Céline thought Streisand was just being polite, her husband and manager, René Angélil, quickly jumped on the invitation. He contacted David Foster, who had worked with both singers, asking Foster to help bring it about. A song entitled "Tell Him" was written expressly for Barbra Streisand and Céline. It features a young woman asking a more experienced woman for relationship advice. The song appeared on Céline's next album, _Let's Talk About Love,_ in 1997.

This particular album would bring famous recording technician Sir George Martin out of retirement to produce the work. Martin became well-known for working in the studio with the Beatles during the pinnacle of their career in the '60s. After working with Céline, Martin said of her, "Céline was a hero and became a friend."

Several duets were planned for the album, including one with Luciano Pavarotti and one with Carole King. But the most important to Céline was the duet with Barbra Streisand. As the only female artist ever to top album charts for four consecutive decades, Streisand's reputation is unequaled.

The "Tell Him" duet was recorded separately with Streisand taping her part first. Céline later recorded her part, using Streisand's tape. "Hearing her voice so close to me, I felt complete," Céline confided later. "I was so close to her breath, her emotion, her soul. I was finally singing with somebody I have been admiring all my life." The chemistry between the two powerful stars impressed even the important recording moguls.

Promotional photographs, taken later, would show the two holding hands, hugging, and clearly showing respect and admiration for each other. The duet was simultaneously featured on a Streisand album, _Higher Ground._ In a clever publicity stunt, Sony delivered the single to radio stations via satellite across North America a full month before the albums were scheduled to hit the stores. The public could hardly wait to

While rumors swirled that Barbra Streisand was upset by Céline's Academy Awards performance, the two divas joined forces on the hit duet "Tell Him."

buy both albums after having heard the single.

During an appearance on the TV talk show *Larry King Live*, Céline told the show host that she admired Streisand for "her singing, her beauty, and her strength." She added enthusiastically that singing with Streisand was "a dream come true."

This "dream come true" as Céline calls it, is only one of a long series of dreams that have come true in her almost magical life. In fact, fellow Canadians nicknamed her "Cinderella Céline."

2

DREAMS START EARLY

Céline Dion was born into a large, happy, musical family on March 30, 1968. Céline's birth received a hearty welcome from eight sisters and five brothers, along with father, Adhémar, and mother, Thérèse. The small town of Charlemagne, Céline's birthplace, lies 30 miles east of Montreal in the province of Quebec, Canada.

Céline's parents met in 1944 at a community dance in the village of La Tuque. The two joined in the jam session with Thérèse playing the violin and Adhémar playing the accordion. Music brought them together, and it was love at first sight. They were married 10 months later, and eventually made their home in Charlemagne

The family quickly grew. With many mouths to feed, Adhémar worked long hours to make ends meet. Both Thérèse and Adhémar grew up as farm children, and both longed to return to the quiet rural life.

The determined couple made a decision to save up money in order to purchase land outside of town. So committed were they to the plan that, rather than take the bus, Adhémar walked to and from the factory where he worked.

Céline, shown here with her father, loved growing up with 13 brothers and sisters. "We had everything we wanted. Love, affection, attention, smart parents, and music. I think that when there is music in your life, there's happiness."

He then put the 40-cent bus fare into a cookie jar. Eventually, they saved enough for a down payment on a plot of land, but there was no money for a house. That did not stop them; they built the house themselves.

In later years, after Céline became famous, the story of her parents' house-building venture became legend in Quebec. Thérèse, pregnant with their seventh child, wielded a hammer, climbed up on a ladder alongside her husband, and banged nails into the roof of their new house. In spite of long hours at the factory, Adhémar worked on the house each night when he came home.

The sacrifice paid off when they moved their family from a small apartment into the comfortable house. It was into this setting that Céline was born. Her musically-minded mother named her after a favorite song which was entitled "Céline."

The basement of the home served as a studio where friends gathered to join in all-night jam sessions. Each of the Dion siblings played several instruments and sang. The basement became Céline's favorite place to be in all the world. Music fed her soul.

Always looking for ways to earn extra money, the family went on the road as a show troupe, calling themselves the Dion Family. Céline has recalled sleeping on the floor of the dressing rooms during the many weekend trips.

As the youngest, Céline was doted upon by her older siblings. Her brother Michel, who later served as Céline's assistant tour director, played in a rock and roll band. He never minded taking his baby sister along on gigs with him. With all this music and the encouragement from her siblings, it's no wonder Céline sang almost as soon as she could talk.

Mimicking the singers she saw on television, Céline had a few moves down pat by age four. Older sister Claudette described Céline using the kitchen table as a makeshift stage, holding a spoon or fork as a pretend microphone. There she serenaded her family. After each song, the adoring audience rewarded her with enthusiastic applause. Céline amazed them with her perfect pitch and with the pure joy she communicated as she sang.

Céline made her first public singing appearance at her brother Michel's wedding in 1973. She sang three songs and stole the show. Everyone who attended the event remembers the awe they felt at hearing the five-year-old execute each song perfectly. It was at that moment that the entire family knew Céline was destined to become a great performer.

Later that same year, a tragic accident nearly robbed the Dion family of their darling baby sister. Usually Céline was never out of the sight of her parents or one of her many brothers or sisters. However, one day she was playing in front of the house near the street while her father and brother Clement worked in the yard. Seeing a baby carriage across the street, she immediately forgot her mother's warning never to cross the street. Loving babies as she did, she wanted to see inside the carriage.

As Céline stepped into the street, the baby's mother yelled for her to stop. Hearing the warning, Céline froze, not knowing what to do next. At that moment a delivery truck backed out of a drive, hit Céline, and threw her into the air. A few feet away, she landed on her head and was knocked unconscious.

It was Michel who reached her first, scooping

her up in his arms and rushing her to the hospital. There Céline lay in intensive care while the family kept close vigil, praying all the while. The doctor warned that Céline might not fully recover. "It was the most devastating time in our lives," Claudette told a reporter later. "Our beloved sister lay in the hospital and there was nothing we could do."

Luckily Céline did pull through, for which the family was deeply grateful. In later years, however, Céline would suffer from intense migraine headaches, which some have attributed to the accident.

Life in the Dion home provided Céline with a safe, happy haven where she enjoyed total contentment. No one seemed to mind that the house was crowded. Brother Jacques remembered how they slept with all five boys in one bedroom. "We stretched out three one way and two another. I had the toes of my brothers in my nose."

With 16 people, even meals were a challenge. Thérèse recalled that each of the children were responsible to wash their own dishes. "Sometimes after dinner we turned the plates upside down for dessert to lessen the burden." Since they did not have a washing machine, Thérèse washed the family clothes in the bathtub.

Having so many children made it difficult to pile everyone in the family car to go visiting. Instead, friends and relatives came to them. The door was always open, and another place at the table was always available. In spite of the financial difficulty, no one seemed to suffer.

"We had everything we wanted," Céline later remembered. "Love, affection, attention, smart parents, and music. I think that when there is music in your life, there's happiness."

Céline couldn't remain in this protective haven forever. Soon it was time for her to go to school. School was a rude awakening for the young singer. Teachers remembered Céline as being shy and withdrawn. Thin and somewhat pale, she took what was dished out by the rough kids, but never retaliated. Because of her prominent front teeth, the other children nicknamed her "the vampire." The painful taunts caused her to dislike school even more.

"I could never answer anything at school anyway," Céline recalled. "School was taking me away from my family and friends and my destiny. Every day I would run home from school as fast as I could. I couldn't wait to come back

Céline grew up outside of a small town like this one about 30 miles from the Canadian city of Montreal in the province of Quebec. She struggled in school, where other children nicknamed her "the vampire" because of her large teeth.

to the basement and hear [my family] rehearse every day."

Céline was uninterested in dolls and toys and school friends. The musical instruments became her toys. Her family provided the friendship. All she ever wanted to do was sing.

With money saved from their family band, Thérèse and Adhémar opened a restaurant and piano bar in Charlemagne, offering patrons food and music. They called the bar Le Vieux Baril (The Old Barrel). Thérèse took charge of the kitchen and Adhémar the front of the restaurant. The kids helped with waiting tables and providing music. Soon Céline was performing as well and became the darling of the customers. Her songs were a mixture of traditional folk ballads and contemporary songs such as those sung by Quebec superstar Ginette Reno. Céline was an avid fan of Reno's.

Soon Céline was practicing for hours before the mirror at home to prepare for her evening performances at the piano bar. Her parents struggled with the dilemma of whether it was right to allow a nine-year-old to hang out at a bar every night. But when not allowed to go, Céline would mope around the house, obviously very unhappy. "I had to let her go to the bar and sing or else she would cry," her mother recalled.

Céline's schoolwork began to suffer. Not because she wasn't bright, but because her mind was back at Le Vieux Baril. Sometimes her siblings helped finish her homework for her so she could go perform. It wasn't very long before customers were planning their evening at the bar around the times when Céline sang. Dozens of phone calls came into the restaurant asking what time Céline would perform and what songs she might be singing.

Offers also began to come in for Céline to perform elsewhere, but that's where her parents drew the line. They felt it was too soon for her to be out from under their watchful eyes. It was Céline's brothers and sisters who encouraged their parents to hurry the process. Brother Jacques suggested they write and record an original song, then place it in the hands of a reputable manager. No one in the family wanted Céline to begin her career in dingy bars and have to work her way up.

Thérèse finally gave in and agreed to team up with Jacques. She wrote the lyrics, and Jacques composed the melody on his guitar. As Céline practiced the song, Thérèse edited the words until it was exactly as she wanted it. The French title "Ce n'était qu'un rêve" translated into English as the perfect theme for Céline's life, "It Was Just a Dream."

Céline sang the song with such emotion and feeling, Claudette cried the first time she heard it. They recorded the song in the family kitchen, using a borrowed tape recorder with Jacques strumming the accompaniment on his guitar. Because singer Ginette Reno was Céline's idol, they decided to send the demo tape to Reno's manager, René Angélil, whose name was listed on the sleeve of an album by the Quebec star.

In order to attract attention, Thérèse wrapped the package up in red ribbon. She also added this note: "This is a twelve-year-old with a fantastic voice. Please listen to her. We want her to be like Ginette Reno."

There was nothing for them to do then but patiently wait.

3

A CHILD STAR

René Angélil was known throughout Quebec not only as a manager, but also as an entertainer in his own right. While still in high school René and two classmates formed a singing group called Les Baronets. The group marketed themselves as Quebec's answer to the Beatles and became highly successful. By the mid-1960s, all their concerts were sellouts. René finally called it quits in 1973 and moved into a second career of managing other musical artists.

René's great drive and sense of ambition led him to produce records for Quebec superstar René Simard as well as managing the career of singing sensation Ginette Reno. He had invested much of his savings into building Reno's career. However, in November 1980, Reno called and told him she no longer needed his services. He had been fired. This news plunged René Angélil into a low point in his entertainment career. He decided that he would begin to study law.

Dozens of young people in Quebec sent tapes to René in hopes of becoming his next big star. The packages remained unopened, including the one wrapped in red ribbon.

Céline Dion and René Angélil pose for photographers in 1995. The first time René heard Céline sing, he was so moved that he cried. Immediately, he became the 12-year-old's manager and eventually guided the gifted singer to international fame.

By mid-January 1981, weary of waiting for a reply, Michel called René, saying he knew René had not listened to the tape as yet, otherwise he would have called the Dions immediately. Soon after Michel's prod, the Dions did receive a call from René's office, saying he wanted to hear Céline in person. A meeting was scheduled at René's Montreal office.

On a cold winter morning, Céline and her mother drove the 30 miles to the city for the interview. Céline, wearing a dress hand-sewn by Thérèse, was nervous. Her mother told her to just be herself. "Sing the way you sing for the people at the bar. You'll be fine."

René remembers Céline as a shy, thin, little girl who was not particularly pretty. He handed her a pen from off his desk and told her to pretend it was a microphone and that she was singing to a crowd of 2,000 friendly people.

The emotion that this 12-year-old girl could pack into a song impressed the manager and moved him deeply. "While I was singing he started to cry," Céline remembered in later years. "I knew then that I had done a good job." René signed her on at that very moment. He promised them that he would make Céline a star within five years. Later he would say what he heard "was the shock of my artistic life."

From the beginning, René took control of Céline's career. He withdrew from his law studies and dropped all other clients. The next step was to mortgage his home to pay for Céline's first recordings. René's wife, Anne (a star of a French-language Canadian TV show), wasn't too happy about that idea, but René's mind was made up. He began hiring the best song writers and setting up recording session dates.

Seeing she could not change René's direction,

Anne agreed to assist. She worked at training Céline on the intricacies of performing. Céline learned from Anne the importance of smiling in public, no matter what. The lesson was well-learned. Later in her life, when Céline became an international star, she was known for her smile, even when she was at her lowest.

René also arranged for Céline to take voice lessons from a famous Quebec vocal coach in addition to piano lessons and her regular schoolwork. Céline threw herself into the music while her schoolwork continued to suffer.

René's idea was to release not one, but two albums from the new unknown singer. He hired the best songwriters, arrangers, and band members for the recordings. The first, *La Voix du Bon Dieu*, consisted of endearing ballads. The next was a Christmas album, *Céline Dion Chante Noël*, which consisted of carols and folk songs aimed at the family market.

By June 1981, through the many connections that he had developed during his years in show business, René arranged for Céline to perform on a popular Quebec talk show. The nervous, frail 13-year-old took the microphone and wowed the television audience. Thus began a love affair between Céline and the people of Quebec which lasts to this day.

The two albums, released in the fall of 1981, sold more than 30,000 copies combined. However, René had been in show business long enough to know that talent alone is not enough to put a star on top—even talent as good as Céline's. Marketing and hard work must also come into play. Céline and René began a grueling schedule of photo shoots, radio and television appearances, and shopping mall gigs. Céline even visited schools, where she signed autographs. She enjoyed talking to school children about the importance of family, her personal disapproval of drugs, and her connection with God. René found Céline to be a trooper when it came to work—her energy seemed to be endless.

Meanwhile, her own schoolwork was falling by the wayside. René hired a tutor for Céline, but she was far more interested in her singing career than in her academic studies. Eventually she would drop out completely at age 15. In 1994 *Time* magazine quoted her as saying that school "was taking me away from music, from my happiness, from my dreams."

As Céline appeared more and more in public, the press made comments about her prominent incisors just as school children had done years before. One humor magazine referred to her as "Canine Dion." Another referred to her as the "vampire kid." These unkind remarks hurt Céline and drove her to tears. She later had her teeth capped, which eliminated the problem altogether.

The next year, Céline flew to France to record a third album with a French record label. The album, *Tellement J'ai D'amour pour Toi* (*I Have So Much Love for You*), became a gold record because of sales in France, and it also sold more than 50,000 copies in Canada. Her acclaim in France prompted Canadian radio shows back home to promote her more.

While she was in Paris, René suggested to Céline that she take additional voice lessons. Their songwriter, Eddie Marnay, took Céline to the home of an elderly lady who had taught opera singers—both men and women. The teacher, Tosca Marmor, was a strict teacher who taught Céline not only about her voice, but

During her first visit to Paris, 14-year-old Céline recorded her third album, which became a major hit in both France and Canada.

also about how to control her emotions.

Later that year, Céline was selected from a field of 2,000 entrants to perform at the 1982 Yamaha World Popular Song Festival in Tokyo. Never had she sung before such a large audience—12,000 in attendance, in addition to 115 million TV viewers.

During the competition, she drew the number five to determine her singing order. The next day, as a finalist, she had to draw another

Céline has always amazed listeners with the power and clarity of her voice. The emotion she conveys often moves them to tears.

number. Again she drew a five.

As she stood backstage (standing so as not to wrinkle the white dress her mother had made) she saw a coin lying on the steps that led to the stage. When she picked it up, she saw it was a Japanese coin with a five on it. She slipped it into her right shoe. From that day forward she believed that five was her lucky number. Céline walked away from this international competition with two awards: Best Song and Best Artist.

Following the festivities, Céline sang another five songs at a private gathering of ambassadors and important Japanese government officials. At the formal banquet, she and her mother sat at the head table.

When Céline returned home from Tokyo, she soon discovered she'd made the front-page news in Quebec. She was greeted by crowds at the airport bearing gifts of stuffed frogs and teddy bears. René Lévesque, the premier of Quebec at the time, personally greeted her and congratulated her. Her fans in Quebec began calling her "p'tite Québécoise" (little Quebecker). In only a scant year and a half she'd become a famous figure in her home country.

Thérèse had accompanied her daughter while she was traveling. The time they spent on the road together helped them get to know one another better than ever before. Thérèse encouraged Céline to keep a diary and record all her impressions of the clean, beautiful country of Japan.

Having Thérèse as her constant companion brought a degree of normalcy to Céline's life. Céline has often said she owes much of her success to the support of her mother. The two remain close.

Céline had no friends her own age simply because of the pace and demands of show business. Her rules for herself were strict: early to bed each night, no cold drinks, no carbonated or alcoholic beverages, and no cigarettes or drugs. Each morning she arose early to practice or to study videos of her past performances. She had no regrets that she had no best girlfriends, wasn't dating, and didn't go to parties. Her dreams were coming true, and that was most important.

When she did have free time, she opted to spend it with siblings and her many nieces and nephews. Family continued to be extremely important, becoming her measuring gauge. Often she asked them to tell her if they saw that she was changing. "I don't want to change," she told them. "I don't want this business to change me."

Céline's fourth single, "D'amour ou D'amitié," sold more copies than the first three singles combined. Continuing her strenuous pace, between 1982 and 1985, she recorded and released nine albums. Her popularity was so great in Canada that in 1985 she received five Félix Awards (Canada's version of the Grammy Awards), shutting out all the competition.

An especially busy year, 1984 saw her singing before an audience of 45,000 at a concert in Montreal. She performed a series of sold-out shows at the famed Olympia Theatre in Paris. In September the entire Dion family was thrilled when Céline was asked to sing before Pope John Paul II during the papal visit to Montreal. Céline sang several songs before the pope and an audience of 65,000 at the Olympic Stadium.

It was also during this time that Céline began donating percentages of concert proceeds to the Cystic Fibrosis Foundation. In 1973 her niece Karine Menard had been born with the incurable disease. The two became very close. Céline loved to take Karine on shopping trips, even if it meant taking along oxygen tanks. Aunt Céline kept promising Karine that they would find a cure for cystic fibrosis, but the chances seemed remote.

By the time Céline turned 17, her success allowed her to purchase a house for her parents in the Montreal suburb of Laval. She then purchased a second home for them in the Laurentian Mountains which overlook the ski resort of Sainte-Anne-des-Lacs. She wanted to reward her parents for all they had done for her through the years.

Céline's next album, *Melanie,* released in 1985, earned her a platinum record in Canada, which meant it sold more than 100,000 copies. That year was marked by a 25-city tour of Quebec in which she performed to standing-room-only crowds at every performance. She was now Quebec's superstar as well as being recognized internationally. Her closet was stuffed with awards, including a total of 15 Felix Awards.

She was concerned, however, that her little-girl image might be an unshakable one. In spite of the fact that she was growing up to be a very beautiful woman, many still thought of her as a child star. René knew the sad track records of many child stars. The attempt to move them into the adult world usually failed. He was willing to do whatever it took to translate Céline's image from a "girlish" one to the adult sphere, and to move her from being a Canadian star into the world market.

Even if they had to take oxygen tanks, Céline loved going on shopping trips with her niece Karine Menard. Karine was born with cystic fibrosis, an incurable disease that usually leads to death by age 30. Céline uses every opportunity to raise money for finding a cure for the disease.

René had an idea of how to accomplish both goals at the same time. His idea was somewhat unorthodox and extremely risky. He asked Céline to suspend her career and public appearances for a full year and a half, during which time she and her image would undergo a total remake. Up until this time, all Céline's songs were recorded only in French. To reach a larger audience, René reasoned, the first item on the "makeover" checklist for Céline was to learn English.

4

COMING OUT

Because of the fast-paced nature of the entertainment business and because of the short memory of the buying public, dropping out of sight meant taking a big gamble. But René was accustomed to gambling. He and Céline agreed this was the only way they could make the needed changes in Céline's image.

Céline enrolled in a Berlitz language school where she attended English classes daily. Because she'd lived in a community where nearly everyone spoke French, she knew only a few phrases in English. The classes proved to be a challenge since the instructors spoke only English. The first few weeks frustrated Céline as she struggled to stop thinking in French and to begin thinking in English. She studied nine hours a day, five days a week for six months. Slowly the ideas and concepts became clearer, and she soon found herself speaking English.

Under René's direction, Céline watched movies in English and listened to a wider variety of music. Her hair was cut short and styled differently. She also went on shopping trips

When Céline signed with CBS Records (later to become Sony) in 1987, no one imagined that she would go on to sell more than 100 million albums. Here in 1999, Sony CEO Tommy Mattola (left) presents her with an award to mark that phenomenal accomplishment.

and learned how to apply makeup professionally. Previously, she'd used little or no makeup since she wanted to appear as "Quebec's child." But that was all changed.

René knew most of the inside workings of show business. He'd worked with people in the music industry most of his adult life, but he'd never met anyone like Céline. Unlike other stars he'd known, Céline was not self-centered. Even though she was the baby of the family and constantly the center of attention, she was not spoiled or selfish. Perhaps it was because she'd been so loved and nurtured that she did not have a deep-seated craving for attention. She was quiet and well-mannered and hungry to learn all she could about becoming a star.

Céline wasn't totally inactive musically during the 18-month break. She released a single in France and a compilation album in Quebec. The latter also gave her a chance to make her first music video.

When it was time for Céline's "coming out," René attempted to renegotiate their contract with Trans-Canada, their original label. However, those in power at the company expressed doubt about the venture. Some even felt that Céline's career was over. They told René that the company was no longer giving cash advances to producers. Without advance money, René could not go forward. It was time to find a new recording company.

René invited the Montreal boss of CBS Records (later to become Sony) along with the CBS promotions manager to a private show in a Montreal hotel. At first the two men told René that Céline's style was all wrong for their company. That was before they saw her performance. Once they heard her, they were convinced: CBS wanted Céline.

A few weeks later, when Céline visited the CBS executive offices, she saw gold and platinum records decorating the walls. One special display caught her eye. A diamond sparkled in the center of the disc. She was told it was for Michael Jackson, who had sold more than a million records in Canada. Silently she wondered to herself if perhaps one day that might happen to her.

Eddie Marnay had served as Céline's personal songwriter in the early years, but she needed new material. New songwriters and new producers came into the picture. Céline's first album with CBS, *Incognito,* was released in April 1987. It represented the first original material she'd recorded in two years. Moving away from ballads, her new music shifted into a heavier beat and bigger sounds, allowing her a more forceful vocal style. The album revealed a new side of Céline. She had emerged a full-grown woman.

Convincing radio stations to play new songs is hard work. René did everything he could to help promote the new album. Single after single climbed the charts in Canada. Céline performed in 42 consecutive sold-out shows in the Saint-Denis Theatre in Montreal. Her comeback was complete and a long list of bookings was soon to follow.

Between tours, Céline loved to go home to be with her family. She especially loved their house in the mountains. Here she could scrub off the makeup, put her hair in a ponytail, don blue jeans, and drive around in her Jeep Cherokee. Her two pet doves and her cat, Isis, were there. The families of her sisters and brothers went in and out in a continuous flow, and sometimes they held impromptu singalongs.

In May 1988, on a visit home, she found that her mother was not feeling well. Céline bundled her mother up, got her into the car, and drove her to the doctor. The doctor insisted her mother be admitted to the hospital right away. That afternoon, Thérèse successfully underwent a quadruple coronary bypass. Relieved that her mother was out of danger, Céline left to star in a concert the very next evening. The incident helped Céline to recognize she was no longer just the baby sister of the family. She could make important decisions and contributions on her own.

In spite of the fact that *Incognito* sold well in France and Canada, Céline was still little known outside those areas. This was soon to change. The Swiss songwriting team of Nella Marinetta and Attila Sereftug had heard Céline's voice, and they were impressed. The two asked her to sing their original song at the Eurovision Song Contest. This famous contest is well known as "Europe's Olympics of song contests." An estimated 600 million TV viewers would be watching.

According to contest rules, only the authors of the song were required to be from the representative country. Thus Céline was not representing France or Canada, but Switzerland. By spring 1988, Céline had made the cut in preliminary Eurovision competitions and was a favorite in the finals. The finals were held April 30 in the huge Simmonscourt studios in Dublin, Ireland.

The suspense following the finalists' performances proved to be almost unbearable. The jury, made up of 16 men and women from several countries, took their time in deliberations.

For a while it looked as though Scott Fitzgerald from England would win. But when the final votes came in, Céline won by one point. Céline, usually cool and collected, was overcome with joy. Her message of thanks, filled with sobs, could barely be understood.

That evening, following the exciting win, René talked to Céline in her room. He explained his impressions of the event as he did after every performance. This night, however, was very different. This night they shared their first kiss as lovers. "My blood changed. I could hear my knees shaking. . . . I knew this was going to be the man of my life," Céline recalled. "The love was so strong, it just took us by storm."

René and Anne had been divorced several years earlier, so there was no reason René and Céline could not have a relationship. However, fearing the fans would not understand their feelings toward each other, the two lovers kept their secret to themselves.

Following the Eurovision win, Céline was at a Dublin press conference where she fielded questions by reporters from all over the world. The British and Irish press featured Céline as the cover story, lauding her vibrant personality and irresistible charm. The win caused her latest album to rack up sales all across Europe. After a short homecoming in Canada, Céline flew back to Europe for a blockbuster promotional tour of a dozen major cities in 10 days. The time was ripe for an album in English.

Her new-found, world-wide celebrity status was not lost on the CBS executives. They poured hundreds of thousands of dollars into her first English album, entitled *Unison*. They pulled in the best producers, one of whom was David Foster. Foster was known for his work with Barbra Streisand, Céline's idol. To top it off, Céline's album was recorded in the same studio where Streisand had recorded many of her successful albums.

Back home in Canada, press reports accused Céline of selling out because she chose to also record in English. Language is extremely important in Quebec. It is, in fact, a hot political issue which Céline tries to avoid as much as possible. Her calm answer to the accusation was, "I want to be—I have to be—known. That's why I'm doing my first English album."

The CBS executives knew Céline's first English album would be a make-or-break venture. If it didn't succeed, the company would lose all the money it had invested in it. For Céline, singing in a new language was a scary experience. So scary, in fact, Céline suffered from a recurring nightmare. In the dream she stands on a narrow ledge high up on a skyscraper. Looking down, she sees swarms of ambulances and police cars. As a police officer reaches out to her, she falls (or jumps, she's never sure which), only to awaken before she hits the sidewalk.

"I have to pretend I am a strong person," she confessed, "but really I am so afraid of making a mistake."

The album was recorded in Los Angeles, New York, and London. Céline's energy and powerful delivery in the recording studios surpassed all expectations. Once the album was released in April 1990, it took off immediately and continued to soar in the United States and worldwide. The album earned her her first gold record in the United States.

The promotions people at CBS arranged for Céline to appear on *The Tonight Show with Jay*

Leno, a highly-popular TV talk show, where she sang a selection from the album, "Where Does My Heart Beat Now?" The show producer was so impressed with her performance, he immediately invited her back for a second appearance.

Continued controversy in Quebec over the English language album led René and Céline to return to the area for a tour to promote *Unison.* On October 13, at the O'Bready Hall in a town called Sherbrooke near the Vermont

Shown here with legendary producer David Foster, Céline has worked hard to achieve success, but it hasn't made her overconfident. "I am so afraid of making a mistake," she's admitted.

border, the unthinkable happened. Céline's beautiful voice broke. She could not finish her show and collapsed backstage.

While she did recover, it remained a frightening experience. The doctor explained that her vocal cords were tired and needed rest. Eventually, a New York throat specialist, Gwen Korovin, whose patients had included Frank Sinatra and Luciano Pavarotti, counseled Céline. Korovin instructed total rest for Céline's voice. To go without speaking was a difficult prescription. But Céline was in this for the long haul. She would do whatever it took. Never again would she take her precious voice for granted.

Some singers turn to drugs to stimulate their voice. Céline chose the more difficult route— the rigors of extreme discipline. She keeps a strict exercise regimen and a strict diet. She uses no drugs and no tobacco, and none of her staff members are allowed to smoke near her the day of a concert. To this day, prior to a concert, Céline rests her voice by not talking. Phoning home to talk to her mother, she taps a code onto the mouthpiece of the phone with her fingernail, a code they have used for many years.

As Céline struggled to save her vocal cords, "Where Does My Heart Beat Now?" continued to climb the charts in America. It remained on the *Billboard* list for 24 weeks and climbed to the fourth position on the Hot 100 Singles list.

With their success bringing in a great deal of money, René and Céline looked for ways to wisely invest her income. They came up with a restaurant-chain idea. Because Céline's lucky number is five, they called the restaurants "Nickels." The first one opened on December 5,

Combining her childhood experiences in her parents' restaurant with her lucky number five, Céline opened a restaurant chain called "Nickels." Each restaurant is built around a '50s theme, complete with jukebox.

1990, in St. Laurent, a Montreal suburb.

The decor consists of a '50s theme with a real jukebox playing oldies and photos on the walls of stars such as James Dean and Elvis Presley. The menu features old-fashioned "comfort" foods, including burgers and thick malts. From the beginning Céline has been active in the company. She even designed the employee uniforms.

Céline's mother owns and operates one of

French-speaking fans in Quebec felt betrayed when Céline released her first English album. To reassure them of her loyalty, she gave concerts throughout Quebec and recorded another French-language album.

the Nickels restaurants, and several of Céline's relatives are employed there. The chain has proved highly successful and looks to expand into Ontario, and eventually into the United States.

Because of the language controversy in Quebec, Céline's next album would once again be sung in French. Hopefully she could prove that she was not turning her back on her French fans. The album was a tribute to Canadian songwriter Luc Plamondon. It went gold in Canada and platinum in France.

International fame appeared to be close at hand when Céline was invited to sing the theme song for a Steven Spielberg movie, *An American Tail: Fievel Goes West.* Well-known singer Linda Ronstadt sang the theme song for the first Fievel film, the story of a brave mouse who sets out to conquer America. However, it seemed Ronstadt was not interested in the sequel.

Céline was invited to record the theme song, entitled "Dreams to Dream." The very words fit her life. The offer thrilled both Céline and René. It wasn't until after Céline actually recorded the song and announced the news to the Canadian press that the deal began to fall apart. Ronstadt had changed her mind, and she had rated high as Spielberg's first pick from the outset. Céline was bitterly disappointed.

As it turned out, the misfortune was a blessing in disguise. Had she recorded the song, a greater opportunity would never have presented itself.

5

DISNEY COMES CALLING

Although the French-speaking Canadians claimed Céline as their very own, she began winning the hearts of those in English-speaking Canada as well. Some looked to her as the one who might reconcile the deep rift between the two groups. In one appearance, she told the English-speaking crowd, "I'm at home right here, onstage. And you're a guest in my home, our home."

Peter North of the *Edmonton Sunday Sun* wrote how he'd been won over by Céline. He referred to her "gracious, charming and sincere personality." He added, "She moves like a moonbeam." To top it off, readers of the popular Canada women's magazine *Chatelaine* voted Céline as one of the 10 most-admired women in 1990. No matter how internationally famous she became, it was important to Céline that she remain connected to her home country.

Céline and René were in London when a director called them with an offer. He told them about a new Disney animated film, *Beauty and the Beast*, which was certain to be a hit. They wanted Céline to sing the theme song. Unlike most kids in the United States, Céline had not grown

---

In the middle of a grueling publicity campaign, Céline's manager, René, suffered a severe heart attack. He recovered, and with the release of her next album, The Colour of My Love, *Céline made public her love for René.*

up around Disney movies. Still hurt over the Spielberg disappointment, she at first appeared uninterested. However, René and his client agreed to fly to Los Angeles to view an unfinished version of the animated film. At the close of the show, Céline jumped from her seat and applauded. Captivated by what she'd seen, she was excited about singing the theme song. It was to be a duet with Peabo Bryson, who was known for singing with such major recording artists as Natalie Cole and Roberta Flack.

While duets can be recorded with one person in the studio at a time, producers felt it important that Céline and Bryson record together. The move was a wise one, as the two worked well together, and the romantic movie theme was an instant hit. And of course, Disney heavily promoted both the movie and the song.

As it turned out in the end, the Fievel movie didn't go very far, and few people even remember the theme song. But "Beauty and the Beast" became Céline's signature song and would make her known throughout the United States, the area she'd worked so hard to break into.

During 1991, Céline enjoyed her first taste of acting. She starred in a Canadian miniseries as a young girl who had been abused by her parents. While she enjoyed acting and hoped to do more, too much of her life was taken up with being the best singer she could be. This left no time for distractions.

The year was capped off with a historical event for Céline. On December 18, she was presented with a contract from Sony (CBS was now called Sony) worth $10 million. It was the biggest contract they had ever signed with a Canadian artist.

Looking back, some observers have said that 1992, instead, was the year that proved to be the turning-point for Céline. In March, she won a Juno Award (an important Canadian musical award) for Female Singer of the Year. In May, she attended the World Music Awards in Monte Carlo, where she received the Best-Selling Canadian Female Artist of the Year Award.

The highlight of the year, however, occurred on her 24th birthday. Since "Beauty and the Beast" was nominated for an Academy Award as Best Original Song, she and Peabo Bryson were scheduled to sing the song live before a TV audience of two billion people.

The massive production number involved a 90-piece orchestra and a large dance troupe. The set was the largest Céline had ever seen. During lengthy rehearsals she stole the hearts of orchestra director Bob Conti and Academy Awards producer Gil Cates. Everyone who met Céline was impressed by her maturity and her warm, happy personality.

On the night of the awards, Céline mingled with famous stars whom she had only dreamed of ever meeting. Back home, Quebeckers were watching and were bursting with pride as Céline gave a flawless performance. As if that were not enough, the song won an Oscar.

"Beauty and the Beast" was featured on Céline's second English album, entitled simply *Celine Dion* (without the accent mark on her name). The album was released the day after the Academy Awards, and she moved into a hectic schedule to promote it. Suddenly, Céline found herself very much in demand; she didn't really belong to herself anymore. April saw her appearing on many of the major talk shows in the United States such as *The Tonight Show with Jay Leno* and *The Oprah Winfrey Show*.

When the Grammy Awards came around,

The release of her album Celine Dion *the day after her duet "Beauty and the Beast" won an Academy Award placed Céline in high demand for appearances on programs such as* The Oprah Winfrey Show. *At times she was so busy that she felt like she didn't belong to herself anymore.*

she and Bryson both took home Grammys for Best Vocal Performance by a Duo. She was also nominated for Female Pop Vocalist of the Year. While she didn't win the Grammy in that category, Céline felt overwhelmed just to be nominated.

In the midst of this fast-paced schedule, on April 29, 1992, René suffered a severe heart attack. The two were resting for a couple of days at a hotel in Los Angeles when the attack struck. Céline immediately took control of the situation and called for an ambulance. She accompanied René to Mt. Sinai Hospital, still clad in her swimsuit. While René made a good recovery, both were shaken by the incident. René began to give thought to the things that truly mattered in his life.

For the first time, Céline was forced to make

appearances without René by her side. She felt lost and alone. She admitted to reporters that René "is my heart. He's the one who makes it beat." She knew she owed everything to this man who had so carefully mapped out her career. And she also knew they were deeply in love.

Being 26 years Céline's senior, René thought if they announced their love relationship, it would ruin Céline's career. He feared the public would see Céline as a home-wrecker, or see him as a fatherly figure, much too old for her. Céline didn't care. Young and in love, she wanted the whole world to know how she felt about René. He convinced her to at least wait until the launch of her next album, and she agreed.

Back into the heavy pace of her work, Céline starred as the opening act for a Michael Bolton tour throughout the summer. This, in addition to the many TV appearances, brought her recognition with the public in the United States. Large companies such as Coca Cola and American Express clamored for Céline to star in their ads.

A song entitled "The Colour of My Love" came to hold a special place in the hearts of Céline and René. It became the title cut of her next album. The song had been written by David Foster for his wife on their wedding day. The moment René heard the song, he loved it and wanted Céline to record it. Every time the two of them heard the song, they wept. Céline found the song so full of love that no matter how many times she sang it, she was overcome with emotion. Later Céline would refer to it as their "forever song, because it's going to be there forever with me."

The Colour of My Love album, released in late 1993, contained another movie theme. "When I Fall in Love," a duet with Clive Griffin, was featured in the hit movie *Sleepless in*

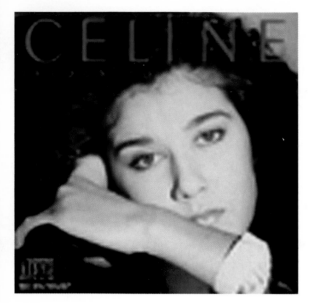

Just six years after the release of Incognito, *her first album with CBS Records, Céline's song "The Power of Love" shot to the top of Billboard's Hot 100 list. It was her first number-one hit in the United States.*

Seattle. Yet another song on the album, "The Power of Love" soared straight to the top of the *Billboard* Hot 100 list and gave Céline her first number-one hit in the United States.

The most important aspect of this special album, however, was not the songs, but rather Céline's personal statement of love to René in the liner notes. The acknowledgments included the following:

René, for so many years I've kept our special dream locked away in my heart . . . but now it's getting too powerful to keep inside . . . so after all these years, let me 'paint the truth, show how I feel' . . . René, you're the color of my love.

At last the secret was out. By the next April, Céline was sporting a sparkling engagement ring. When Thérèse was first told of the couple's intentions she admitted, "I reacted badly." The age difference between the two greatly concerned Céline's mother. However, since Thérèse had always respected and admired René, she later softened. The couple received her blessings.

Céline jumped into the New Year by singing for the president of the United States, Bill Clinton, during his January 1993 "Celebration for Youth" gala at the Kennedy Center in Washington, D.C. Later that winter, she sang at the American Music Awards.

In March *Billboard* magazine presented her with a special prize. To celebrate her achievements around the world, they gave her the Billboard International Creative Achievement Award. Following that exciting event, she

hosted the Juno Awards ceremony in Canada, during which
she received four awards and
sang two songs.

"My life is a fairy tale, and I
know it," she said. And she was
right.

The monumental year was
also shadowed by deep sadness.
Céline watched helplessly as
her niece Karine grew weaker
and weaker. In spite of all the
thousands of dollars Céline
poured into the Canada Cystic
Fibrosis Foundation, there was
still no cure for Karine or the

others who suffered from this crippling disease.

In May, as soon as she returned from London,
Céline rushed to the hospital to see Karine. "I've
been waiting for you," the 16-year-old told her
aunt. She wanted to change into a pair of fresh
pajamas. René rushed out and purchased three
pairs. With Karine's mother's help, Céline helped
Karine change into her new pajamas. Then
Céline sang to her.

*Celine Dion Celebrity
Chocolates are only
one way Céline uses
her fame to benefit
charities. Sales of the
candy raise money
for music programs
in public schools.*

Karine began to talk about all the good
things in her life that she could remember.
Soon after, she died right in Céline's arms.
Four years later, Céline stated, "I love Karine
very much, she's still with me." Céline stepped
up her charity concerts for cystic fibrosis, rais-
ing hundreds of thousands of dollars for the
cause. Karine would never be forgotten.

In November, at the launch of *The Colour of
My Love* album in Montreal, Céline announced
that she and René would be married. As he
joined her on the stage at the Métropolis in
front of 2,500 special guests and the many TV

viewers, they kissed in public for the first time. The place erupted in cheers. All René's fears had been for nothing.

One newspaper announced, "It isn't only Mama Dion who is marrying off a daughter. It's all of Quebec."

Less than two weeks after *The Colour of My Love* hit the stores, it had gone platinum in Canada and five times platinum in the United States. This was definitely the album that would turn the tide of her entire career. René knew it was time for them to move into the merchandising aspect of the business, including Céline T-shirts, caps, jackets, signed photos, programs, and other memorabilia. The fans snapped them up as soon as they were in the stores.

Just as Céline had planned every detail of her tours, she planned every detail of her wedding. All her life she'd dreamed of a fairy-tale wedding. Theirs would be exactly that.

The event took place on December 17, 1994, in an intimate ceremony for 500 guests at the Notre Dame Basilica in Montreal. A motorcade of 17 limousines carried the wedding party to the church. Céline's brothers and sisters serenaded her with a song composed especially in honor of the couple. As Céline walked down the aisle, a string orchestra played *their* song, "The Colour of My Love."

Céline's dress, which followed her specific design, required hundreds of hours of custom sewing. Céline wanted a traditional dress with fan-shaped sleeves, a tiny fitted waist, and massive skirt. The headdress was created from 2,000 Austrian crystals. The final fitting occurred only two days before the wedding.

A reception after the exchange of vows featured a five-course dinner followed by an

Céline had always dreamed of a fairy-tale wedding, so her nuptials included everything from 17 limousines for the wedding party to a wedding cake made of 2,000 pastries. At the press conference after the reception, Céline's joy was obvious to everyone.

enormous wedding cake made of 2,000 pastries arranged in the shape of a Christmas tree. During the press conference held after the reception, everyone could see that Céline was giddy with joy. She laughed and giggled and pretended to swoon into René's arms. The day she'd waited for and dreamed of was hers at last. To her, their wedding day was more important than any award she'd ever received.

6

TITANIC!

Céline wasted no time in getting back to work. In 1995, she collaborated with a famous French songwriter, Jean-Jacques Goldman, to produce an album in French, *D'eux*. The sales surprised everyone. In only seven months it became the best-selling French music album in history. In Britain, it became the first French album to go gold, staying on top for 44 weeks.

Before the year was out, Céline made headway even in Japan. She recorded a song entitled "To Love You More" to be used as a theme song for a Japanese TV drama series. The single sold 1.3 million copies, making it the first foreign song to reach the top of the Japanese charts in 12 years.

Back in North America, "Because You Loved Me," the theme song from the movie *Up Close and Personal*, was the first single to be released from Céline's fourth English album, *Falling into You*. Céline's voice was heard every time the movie ads aired. *Falling into You* became the most successful release of Céline's career. It shot to first place on the *Billboard* Hot 200 list and remained in the top four for 27 consecutive

---

Céline's performance at the 1999 Billboard *Music Awards was one of her last public appearances before taking a planned two-year break from her career. Learning of René's battle with cancer, few fans questioned Céline's decision, but they were united in missing her charismatic stage presence.*

weeks. Worldwide it smashed records in France, England, Switzerland, Belgium, the Netherlands, Norway, Austria, and Australia. The *Falling into You* two-year tour took her around the world.

As a true international star, it was no surprise when Céline was invited to sing at the opening ceremonies of the 1996 Olympics in Atlanta. There she performed a song written especially for the occasion, "The Power of the Dream," a song that fit her life perfectly. She'd seen what the power of a dream could really do. Singing live before an audience of approximately 3.5 billion TV viewers all around the world, she executed the song perfectly.

The year was filled with a dizzying schedule of tours, TV appearances, radio interviews, and charity concerts. René kept up with every press release, review, and article written about Céline. Nothing slipped past his attention. He carefully selected which invitations to accept and which to turn down.

Céline, on the other hand, never seemed to be bothered by rumors or "bad press." René marveled that she could be so detached, but her focus was to sing and to sing well. While an interview might unnerve her, she was most at home on the stage. She wasn't so much interested in hit albums as in an ongoing career.

Challenges that once seemed insurmountable to Céline now came easily. Sometimes she missed the challenges. That's why she was particularly happy to be invited to sing the second number at the Academy Awards ceremony in March 1997. There was something about the scariness of it all that excited Céline and appealed to her sense of adventure.

Money accompanied Céline's fame. In 1997 she made the *Forbes* magazine list of top-paid entertainers. At $65 million, her income topped even that of her idol Barbra Streisand.

In the world of opera, the female lead singer is sometimes referred to as a *diva,* or the star. The media has attached the title of diva to several famous singers of the day. However, for Céline, it's different. Céline is known as the "global diva" or the "international diva."

In the summer of 1997, Céline discovered the game of golf and loved it. Finally, she had a sport to serve as a diversion from her busy life. She enjoyed the challenge of the game so much she bought her own golf course. Céline is also a fan of pro golfer Tiger Woods. "He's not only the No. 1 golfer, he's the No. 1 human being," Céline said of Woods. She often attended Tiger Woods's charity events for disadvantaged youths.

Meanwhile out in Hollywood, an epic movie was in production. The film, *Titanic,* was over budget and behind schedule. While some saw the project as a loser, director James Cameron held unwavering faith in it. James Horner, a friend of Céline's and René's, was working on the music for the film. Cameron had told Horner that a pop tune was not acceptable for this type of movie, but Horner disagreed.

Without telling Cameron, Horner presented "My Heart Will Go On," the theme song of the film, to Céline and René. In spite of Horner's less-than-professional presentation of the song, Céline liked it and agreed to record a demo.

Horner waited more than a month before playing the demo for Cameron. When he did, Cameron was quite impressed. In fact, he loved the song and Céline's singing so much he didn't want a retake. Everyone agreed. The first take was a magic moment. No one wanted to tamper with perfection. Not only did the song become

The two Grammy Awards Céline won for her Titanic *hit "My Heart Will Go On" reflect her technical excellence as a singer, but fans love Céline as much for her warmth and charm.*

identified with the immensely popular movie, it was also included on Céline's next album, *Let's Talk About Love.*

No one could have known what an impact *Titanic* would make on moviegoers everywhere. The movie stayed in the number one box-office spot for 15 weeks and became the biggest grossing film of all time. The *Titanic* soundtrack became as popular as Céline's album. It broke a *Billboard* record, selling 500,000 copies for six consecutive weeks in America, and became the best-selling film score of all time. The movie captured 11 Academy Awards, one of which was Best Original Song. Everything Céline Dion touched seemed to turn to gold.

Having won nearly all the awards that the music industry could offer, what was left?

Canada had the answer. On April 30, 1998, Céline was awarded the Order of Quebec. The next day, May 1, she was awarded the Order of Canada. These are the highest honors given to Quebeckers and Canadians. Because of the strong divisions between Quebec and the rest of the country, Céline stated she was proud to be a Quebecker and equally proud to be a Canadian.

No matter where in the world Céline travels, she makes friends. People who meet her never forget her. She has a way of making everyone feel equal. Many stars come across to their fans either as martyrs with sad stories and many regrets or as arrogant snobs. Céline, on the other hand, lets her audiences know how happy she is and what a wonderful life she leads.

People love Céline not only because she is warm and real, but because she sings about love. She sings as a statement, but never as a protest. David Platel, René's right-hand man, says about Céline: "She never tries to get your attention by shocking you with far-out or disturbing ideas. She conquers you with her voice, her charm and by projecting a simple, balanced way of life."

Céline talked about taking a break for over a year. No one really believed her, especially when, in early 1999, she launched a worldwide tour and released a new album, *All the Way . . . A Decade of Song*. The album is a collection of her greatest hits and it includes several new songs. However, suspending her musical career took on a greater sense of urgency when her husband was diagnosed with cancer in April 1999.

In the midst of a hectic concert tour, René felt a bulge in his throat. Céline, who is obsessive about throat problems, was very concerned. The next day, at Céline's insistence, René went for a checkup. The doctor reported that the bulge was a cancerous growth and it "doesn't look good." He scheduled René for surgery that very night.

Céline could not cancel her concert that night, but she rushed to the hospital the next day. René reported that he could not eat or swallow. Oddly enough, it was Céline's 31st birthday. On that day, she changed from René's protégée to his caretaker. She immediately canceled her upcoming concert dates, clearing her schedule for about a month. "I was there for him, and I felt great about it," she said of their instantaneous role reversal. "I was so proud of the way I reacted," Céline told one reporter. "I became so strong, so in charge, so in control."

Céline accompanied her husband every time he went for radiation treatments. "There is not a word that exists that can express how much I love her," René has said. Céline saw what happened to René as life sending her a message. "The message was . . . Show business is not your life. . . . It's about time you do something else. It's time that you are there for each other, that you get back into reality, be with your family and friends," she expressed.

Before beginning her two-year break, Céline said her good-byes in a taped one-hour concert which aired on CBS on November 24, 1999. She then gave two farewell concerts: one on New Year's Eve in Montreal, and the other on January 1, 2000 in Las Vegas, Nevada.

Summing it all up, Céline said, "When I look back over the past ten years, I can't believe what an incredible journey it has been. I have so many things to be grateful for . . . so many great memories. . . . So much has happened and I feel so very fortunate that I've been able to live this

Céline shares a moment with René after unveiling her star on the Canadian Walk of Fame in 1999. Having survived René's heart attack and cancer treatments, the couple sees each day they spend together as a gift to be treasured.

dream. There's still a lot more that I want to do in music . . . which I hope to pursue in time. For now, I want to step back a little bit . . . to enjoy the simple things in life for a change . . . to spend more time with my family, my friends and especially with René."

The billions of people who have witnessed and been inspired by Céline's heartfelt and dynamic performances are sad to see her go. But ever since she was a tiny girl, Céline has been a person on the move—following her heart and making things happen.

She shows no sign of changing anytime soon!

CHRONOLOGY

1968	Born on March 30 in Charlemagne, Quebec.
1973	First public appearance, singing at brother's wedding.
1981	René Angélil becomes Céline's manager.
1982–85	Records nine albums in French, seven in Quebec and two in France.
1982	Wins the Yamaha World Popular Song Festival in Tokyo.
1984	Sings before Pope John Paul II and an audience of 65,000 during the pope's visit to Montreal, Canada.
1986	Begins 18-month break from public to study English and reconstruct her image.
1987	Unveils new image; signs with CBS; *Incognito* is released.
1988	Wins the Eurovision competition in Dublin, Ireland.
1990	Opens first Nickels restaurant in Montreal; releases first album in English.
1991	Signs a $10 million contract with Sony.
1992	Records the theme song for movie *Beauty and the Beast.*
1993	CBS releases *The Colour of My Love* album; announces her love for manager, René Angélil; niece Karine Menard dies of cystic fibrosis.
1994	Marries René Angélil.
1996	Sings at opening ceremonies of summer Olympics in Atlanta.
1997	Sings two songs at the Academy Awards in Los Angeles; two-year, worldwide tour begins; records the *Titanic* theme song "My Heart Will Go On."
1998	Becomes an Officer of the Order of Canada and of the Order of Quebec.
1999	René is treated for cancer; Céline performs "farewell" concert on CBS; performs at the first of two pre-hiatus concerts on New Year's Eve in Montreal.
2000	Performs at the second of two pre-hiatus concerts on New Year's Day in Las Vegas.

DISCOGRAPHY

Top Singles

1990   "Where Does My Heart Beat Now"

1992   "Love Can Move Mountains"
         "If You Asked Me To"
         "Water from the Moon"

1993   "Beauty and the Beast" (*Beauty and the Beast* theme song)

1994   "When I Fall in Love" (*Sleepless in Seattle* theme song)

1996   "Because You Loved Me" (*Up Close & Personal* theme song)
         "It's All Coming Back to Me Now"
         "All by Myself"
         "The Power of the Dream" (theme song for the Olympics)

1997   "Tell Him" (duet with Barbra Streisand)
         "My Heart Will Go On" (*Titanic* theme song)

1999   "That's the Way It Is"

Albums (French)

1981   *La Voix du Bon Dieu*
         Céline Dion Chante Noël

1982   *Tellement J'ai D'amour pour Toi*

1985   *Melanie*
         C'est pour Toi

1987   *Incognito*

1993   *Les Premieres Années*

1995   *D'eux*

1998   *S'il Suffisait D'aimer*

Albums (English)

1990   *Unison*

1992   *Celine Dion*

1993   *The Colour of My Love*

1996   *Falling into You*

1997   *Let's Talk About Love*

1998   *These Are Special Times*

1999   *All the Way . . . A Decade of Song*

AWARDS

American Music Awards

Billboard Music Awards

Blockbuster Entertainment Awards

Canadian Academy for Recording Arts and Sciences Awards

Diamond Awards

Felix Awards

Grammy Awards

Irish Recorded Music Awards

Juno Awards

MetroStar Awards

Midem Awards

Much Music Awards

Order of Canada

Order of Quebec

People's Choice Awards

VH-1 Awards

World Music Awards

FURTHER READING

Alexander, Charles P. "The Power of Celine Dion," *Time*, March 7,1994.

Cole, Melanie. *Céline Dion*. Childs, MD: Mitchell Lane Publishers, Inc., 1998.

Crouse, Richard. *The Celine Dion Story: A Voice and a Dream*. New York: Ballantine Books, 1998

Dean, Jeremy. *Celine Dion: Let's Talk About Love*. New York: Welcome Rain, 1998.

Germain, Georges-Hébert. *Céline Dion: The Authorized Biography of Céline Dion*. Toronto: Dundurn Press, 1998.

Halperin, Ian. *Céline Dion: Behind the Fairytale*. Boca Raton, FL: Boca Publications Group, Inc., 1997.

Law, Kevin. *Canada*. Philadelphia: Chelsea House Publishers, 1999.

McKay, Marianne. *Celine Dion*. New York: MetroBooks, 1999.

ABOUT THE AUTHOR

NORMA JEAN LUTZ, who lives in Tulsa, Oklahoma, has been writing professionally since 1977. She is the author of more than 250 short stories and articles as well as 39 books—fiction and nonfiction. Of all the writing she does, she most enjoys writing children's books.

INDEX